Pontefract

IN OLD PHOTOGRAPHS

Pontefract

IN OLD PHOTOGRAPHS

Compiled by
RICHARD VAN RIEL

ALAN
SUTTON

Alan Sutton Publishing Limited
Phoenix Mill · Far Thrupp
Stroud · Gloucestershire

Published in collaboration with

City of Wakefield
Metropolitan District Council

First published 1993

British Library Cataloguing in Publication Data

Richard Van Riel
Pontefract in Old Photographs
I. Title
942.815

ISBN 0–7509–0337–6

Typeset in 9/10 Sabon.
Typesetting and origination by
Alan Sutton Publishing Limited.
Printed in Great Britain by
Redwood Books, Trowbridge.

Contents

Gardiner's window-cleaning service in front of Maud's Yard, off Market Place. Signs for the Central Studio (Maud's Photographers) are visible, as well as evidence of transport by tram and by horse.

Introduction

The rich and varied history of Pontefract is well served by an abundant survival of photographs. This collection covers two main periods of change. First, the turn of the century when the town's population tripled with the growth of mining, liquorice and the Barracks; and second, the redevelopment during the 1960s when many fine buildings were demolished. The photographs also hint at the borough's much older past – the turbulent history of the Castle and the monasteries and markets which made Pontefract the main centre of West Yorkshire in the Middle Ages. The town which grew in the shadow of the powerful Castle was granted its first charter as early as 1194.

Local pride has led to the preservation of an unusually rich photographic archive. The formal studio and business photographs of Maud's Photographers contrast with the topical pictures of events and people from the *Pontefract Advertiser*. A vivid picture of institutional life is given by the lantern slide collection of Pontefract workhouse.

The archive has continued to expand thanks to the foresight of groups such as the Pontefract Archaeological Society and individuals such as Eric Houlder, Harry Battye, Don Lodge and John Holmes who have recorded the changing town from the 1950s onwards. In addition Peter Cookson has meticulously chronicled rail transport in the area over the past forty years. When you take into account the already published collections of the Kinsley evictions (a rare survival of industrial history) and the magnificent work of Jack Hulme in photographing the mining village of Fryston, it will be seen that Pontefract's photographic heritage is rich indeed. The museum is always interested in recording for posterity photographs from family albums which fill gaps in the existing collections.

Collecting the town's photographs has been one of the most rewarding parts of my work since the museum opened in 1978. I hope that readers of this book will now be able to share that pleasure.

Richard Van Riel
Curator of Pontefract Museum
City of Wakefield Metropolitan District Council
Museums, Galleries and Castles

The new post office being built on Ropergate. The architects, Garside and Pennington, designed many other buildings in the town, including the Free Library, the Alexandra Theatre, and the Greyhound and the Golden Ball public houses.

SECTION ONE
The Changing Town

Market day at the turn of the century (pre-1902), before the bay-fronted building was demolished to make way for Blackburn's furnishings.

Pontefract Market Hall before the frontage was altered and then lowered. The pediment, stone balustrading, lantern and ventilation louvres are visible. This grand building was opened in 1860 by Viscount Palmerston.

This fine three-storey building on Market Place was probably built around 1725. Its design, like the Mansion House in York, was modelled on the Banqueting Hall, Whitehall.

Market Day in 1906. On the right the shop goods from Wordsworth's and England's ironmongers spill out on to the pavement.

Cycling through the market, *c.* 1940. Mind the dog!

The post office on Market Place. Built in 1887, it was closed in 1915 and later demolished to make way for Valley Road.

A demolition gang working on the new Valley Road in 1938.

The Shoe Market around the turn of the century, with the sign of the old Cross Keys on the left.

Shillaker's shop front on the corner of Beastfair and the Ginnel leading to Shoe Market. Hams hung outside. The drum-shaped cheeses were vulnerable to passing dogs.

Beastfair in the nineteenth century. The publican's name, Walshaw, on the prominent sign and the lack of a post office at the end of the road places this photograph between 1866 and 1887. The unattended goat is a reminder of how rural the area around the town centre must have been.

The Cornmarket before the War Memorial was resited. The complete frontage of the White Hart can be seen.

Beastfair, looking north. Joseph Dawson's small fishmonger's shop in the foreground contrasts with its three-storied neighbour, Thomas Wordsworth, grocer and provision dealer.

A tram on Cornmarket passing the law courts on the way to Castleford and Normanton.

Beastfair, 1906. Note the woman wearing the straw hat in front of the Malt Shovel.

Star Yard off Beastfair. The flags and decorations celebrate Queen Victoria's Diamond Jubilee in 1897.

Ornate fireplace and overmantel from Blackburn's Outfitters, Beastfair (now Boots).

The completed new post office, 1915. The shop front in the foreground prominently displays a recruitment poster.

Street life in Ropergate at the turn of the century. In the distance the old post office and the Market Hall can be seen.

Town End, looking up Wakefield Road. In the foreground is the New Inn, which was rebuilt in around 1936 and finally demolished for Jubilee Way.

Town End pre-1896, looking towards Southgate. On the right is a tollhouse, which was replaced by Ewbank's garage.

Widening Southgate in 1938.

Horse trough and gas lamp by the Valley Cafe at the bottom of Mill Hill, c. 1950.

Timber-framed buildings on Newgate, dating from the sixteenth and seventeenth centuries, seen from the back.

Timber-framed buildings on Newgate. Notice the cart-sized entrance to Leng's Yard, also called Playhouse Yard.

Bullock's pot shop at the junction of Front Street and Back Street. This timber structure was demolished to give clearance for the trams soon after 1906.

The stone ladder leads to a loft in a yard off Newgate. Part of the Crescent cinema can be seen through the arch.

The junction of Ropergate End with Newgate. This area was demolished for Jubilee Way.

Looking down Mill Hill when it was a peaceful lane. Underground sand quarries were reached from doors in the overhang. Note the First World War poster.

The busy junction of Bridge Street, Wool Market, Market Place and Gillygate, *c.* 1890.

Wool Market, looking towards the Town Hall, which was designed by Bernard Hartley in 1785. The shops on the right were demolished around 1936.

Great Northern House was demolished in 1973 to create access from the redeveloped Salter Row to the new extension to Stuart Road.

Horsefair, *c.* 1910.

Horsefair from the top, looking downhill. The width of the street reminds us that this was the main street (or Micklegate) and site of the market until the new Market Place was added in the twelfth century.

Gardiner's House, Horsefair, now demolished. Some of its seventeenth-century oak panelling can be seen in Pontefract Museum.

Ornate plaster ceiling in Gardiner's House. The same plasterer was probably responsible for the ceiling in the parlour of Clarke Hall, Wakefield, dated 1680.

Micklegate House, Horsefair, demolished as part of the Poulson redevelopment scheme. The original eighteenth-century building was probably extended by John Carr.

Ornate plaster ceiling and fireplace in Micklegate House by Giuseppe Cortese, who was working in Yorkshire around 1725.

The corner of Baxtergate and Bridge Street. The spur of houses projecting downhill from the Town Hall was still a feature on the 1891 Ordnance Survey map.

South Baileygate when the road was still quiet enough for children to play in.

Tanner's Row corner with South Baileygate. The snicket led to gardens and orchards behind the houses.

A rear view of houses in the Booths area.

The interior of one house in the Booths area.

Yards and sheds behind the houses on South Baileygate.

The Booths, looking uphill, *c.* 1940.

'Paddy's Hall', a one-up one-down,
which was cleared with other houses
in the Booths area around 1965.

New Hall, *c.* 1890. It was built by Robert Smythson in 1591 using stones from St John's priory.

New Hall, *c.* 1905. By 1965 New Hall was considered unsafe and was blown up with dynamite. The stone was reused in the foundations of the Wentbridge viaduct.

This Tanshelf shop photograph was used to send Christmas greetings. The photograph must have been taken near election time as somebody has chalked Vote Labour on the brickwork.

SECTION TWO
Tanshelf and Carleton

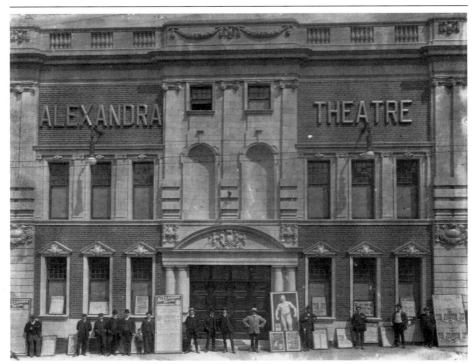

The Alexandra Theatre, designed by George Pennington. It was converted into a cinema in 1936.

An Alexandra Theatre billboard advertising the fight between Johnson and Burns.

The corner of Front Street and Stuart Road.

Colonel's Walk, Tanshelf, looking downhill towards the Prince of Wales pit, *c*. 1940.

Wilcock's bakery between Anderson Street and Nut Street in Tanshelf. The bakery was popular with children who could buy cake bits at 1d a bag.

The Queen's Hotel, looking up Front Street.

Battye's newsagents, Tanshelf.

The Ackworth Road junction with Carleton Road, looking towards Mill Hill. Bar Terrace on the right was named after the turnpike tollhouse which stood there.

Carleton Road, *c.* 1930. The village of Carleton was developing into a suburb.

The timber parish hall on Carleton Green was demolished in 1990.

Carleton Players in front of the Rookeries, *c.* 1890.

Hockey players below the Rookeries, *c.* 1940.

Children from the orphanage at Eastwell Lodge posing on the village green around 1910.

Children from Eastwell Lodge peeling potatoes and cleaning cutlery, *c.* 1910.

The one and only Leidart at Carleton Green. Built by Mr Leith and Mr Huddart in Cornmarket, the car had a 3.6-litre V8 engine.

Midhall, Carleton. The car has the unusual number plate of WR 1.

Fairfax's cottage, Carleton, where General Fairfax is reputed to have had his headquarters during the sieges of Pontefract Castle which took place between 1644 and 1648. It later became a dame school before being demolished.

The old Roman Catholic Mission chapel of St Michael the Archangel stood on the edge of Carleton Green until it too was demolished.

The Grange, Carleton, rebuilt in the 1870s by the banker, Thomas Tew. The entrance porch is visible in this photograph.

A rear view of The Grange, Carleton, with the orangery on the left. Both buildings were protected from cattle by a ha-ha (dry ditch).

Pontefract Mace Bearer Abraham Baxter, *c.* 1880.

SECTION THREE

The Borough

Horse-drawn fire engines were in use in Pontefract up to the 1920s.

Mayor F.W. Pease with the fire brigade in 1899 or 1900. The fire engine was kept under the Town Hall arch.

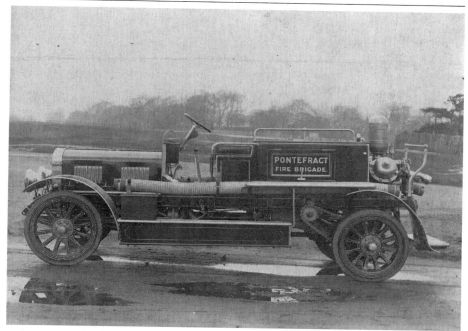

The new motorized fire engine, *c.* 1921.

The fire engine with its extending ladder at the corner of Gillygate and Market Place.

Roall Waterworks. The ceremony of cutting the first sod took place on 25 June 1889. Roall and Eggborough Waterworks became Pontefract's main suppliers of water.

Pontefract's old waterhouse on Wakefield Road. The building was demolished in 1933.

St Ives' Well, off Spittal Hardwick Lane. This well was probably dedicated in the Middle Ages but was recently ploughed over.

Tanshelf pumping station and elevated tank. The Tanshelf works were started in 1852.

Pontefract Park water tower under construction. It was completed in 1929.

Staff inside the underground reservoir on Park Hill in 1929.

Constable Jack Drewett, who was in the Pontefract Borough Police from 1876 to 1902. He was famous for patenting a new felt sock for strenuous walkers!

Pontefract's first workhouse in Micklegate, c. 1960, before the Back Northgate complex was built.

Sessions House, Cornmarket, designed in Ionic style by Charles Watson in 1807.

The infirmary block built for the workhouse off Back Northgate. The building, designed by Tennant and Smith, can be seen here with the grounds yet to be completed.

Compacted waste paper being carted away from the 'destructor' on Headlands Road. Its furnaces used to incinerate the refuse and the heat generated by the process warmed the water for the swimming pool across the road.

Sawing logs at Pontefract workhouse, *c.* 1910.

Pontefract workhouse, *c.* 1910. This man is breaking stones for use in road building.

Splitting logs at Pontefract workhouse, *c.* 1910. Various forms of hard labour were organized to help pay for the upkeep of the inmates and also to act as a deterrent in the unlikely event that someone saw life in the workhouse as an easy option. Ironically its address was Paradise Close or Paradise Fields.

Samuel Hirst, farmer, land valuer and first chairman of the Board of Guardians of the new workhouse. Hirst is famous for his very full diaries which he kept from 1831 to 1880.

Pontefract Corporation Road Construction Unit, *c.* 1901. Mr T. Hopkinson is at the wheel of the steam roller.

Mayor Thomas Routlidge, 1852.

Mayor Roger Hurst (mayor in 1850, 1861 and 1862).

Mayor Robert Arundel, 1865.

Mayor John Rhodes (mayor from 1880 to 1886 and 1889 to 1890). He was responsible for the sinking of the Prince of Wales pit between 1869 and 1874.

A rainy day in Ropergate, *c.* 1950.

SECTION FOUR

Shopping

The Maypole on Beastfair and its staff.

Bullock's pot shop on Horsefair, *c.* 1890.

Woolworth's Saturday girls with their 'floor walker', Gladys Ellis, *c.* 1937.

Seaton's Noted Toffee stall outside England's ironmongers, *c.* 1920.

Naitby's Pure Ices, Northgate.

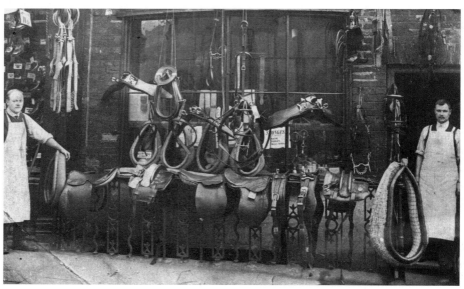

P. Chapman and Son, saddlers, Beastfair. The horse collar on the right was reputed to be the largest in England.

T.M. Barker's float in front of St Joseph's School on Love Lane. Beware the walking Vimto bottle!

Gardiner's of Cornmarket, trying to win the best dressed window competition. Note the fish displayed in a block of ice.

Queen Mary shopping at Farr's Antiques on Castle Chain.

An advertising card for Farr's Antiques, established 1866.

The Fifty Shilling Tailors, Market Place, *c.* 1920. Note the medieval jettied buildings with Georgian modernizations of bay window and columns.

Interior of Vaux Brothers, family grocers, *c.* 1920. The shop closed on 27 July 1973.

Ewbank & Son, car and cycle showroom, Town End, *c.* 1910.

The art deco frontage of Keyzers, Ropergate, *c.* 1930.

The Public Benefit Boot Company, Cornmarket, *c.* 1907. Mr Greasley is seen with his assistant, Miss Spurr.

Wordsworth's grocers, *c.* 1930. The building also housed a famous ballroom.

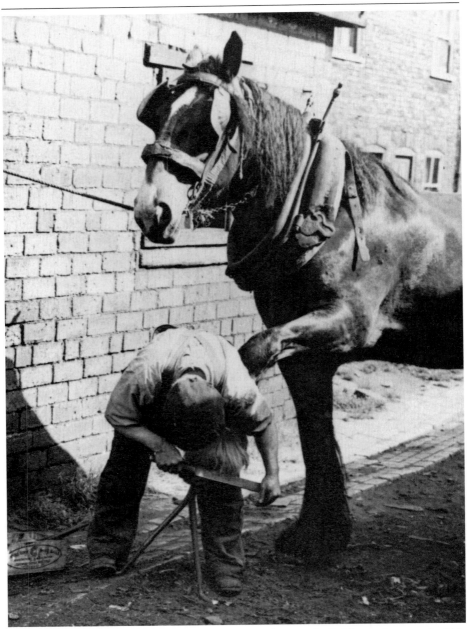

Farrier Joe Richardson at work in Crown and Anchor Yard. Children often watched his skilful work, partly to see if the horse would bite his backside, which occasionally it did.

SECTION FIVE

Trades and Professions

The skinyards of the Co-operative Wholesale Society, South Baileygate. Jabez Crashley is pulling on the fleshing knife; note how his whole body is balanced on his stomach muscles.

CWS skinyard workers sorting wool into suspended sacking, *c*. 1930.

Waddington's skinyards which were later taken over by CWS. Mr Waddington is in the white jacket. The men with poles are dipping the skins in the Wash beck which was channelled through the yards.

Gardiner's industrial vacuum cleaner in operation at the Red Lion Hotel, Market Place.

Charles Askew with his rescue kit in front of the Prince of Wales pit.

Bradburn's Pure Ices in Maud's Yard.

A photograph by Mr Maud of two difficult subjects: a child and a dog. The hand would have been edited out afterwards.

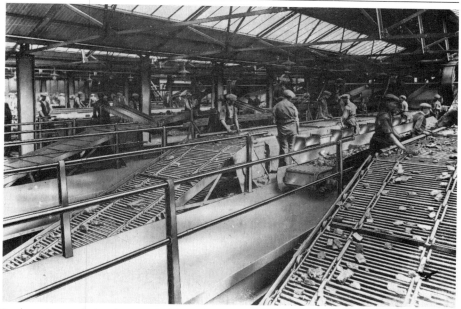

Coal sorting and cleaning, probably at the Prince of Wales pit, around 1910.

Underground at the Prince of Wales pit, *c.* 1920. Note the timber props and nearly round shovel.

The Penny Bank, Ropergate, c. 1910. Sadly this fine building was demolished.

The ornate Midland Bank, Ropergate, complete with its railings and iron balconettes.

The lamplighter at work, probably on Southgate, *c*. 1950.

Ninety-year-old William Wilcox, carpenter, decorating his home. He built a wooden model of All Saints' double helix staircase. Note the over-trousers.

Staff of Charles Farr's furniture restoration workshop off Ropergate. Mr Farr is in the centre with his hands in his pockets.

Staff of Abbot's Funeral Directors and Carpenters, photographed on the corner of Dark Lane and Mill Hill.

The Belvedere Studio, St Bernard's Avenue. Mr Hewes set up his business by the Barracks to specialize in regimental group photographs and single portraits of soldiers in uniform for families and sweethearts.

Three generations of Cawthornes tailoring in Finkle Street.

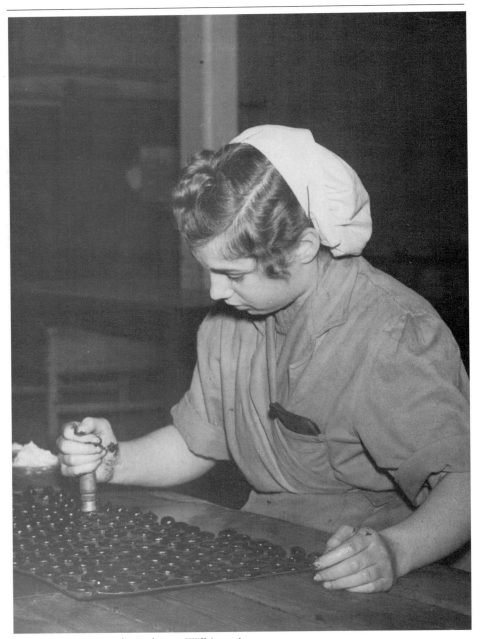

Hand stamping Pomfret cakes at Wilkinson's.

SECTION SIX

Liquorice

Friarwood when it was a mixture of liquorice and orchards. Note the ladder for fruit picking.

Thomas Glover digging a liquorice grip (or trench) in the area of the Valley Gardens.

Valley Gardens before it became a park.

Looking down from the Blue Bell steps when there were still liquorice, orchards and market gardens.

Wroe's liquorice factory in 1902. Note the age range of the workers.

Workers at Wilkinson's liquorice factory. Few men were employed in sweet production.

Wilkinson's old factory, *c*. 1910.

Wilkinson's new factory under construction. It was designed by Tennant and Smith and opened in 1947.

Ernest Whincup and his horse, Tinker, transporting wooden liquorice boxes on the Wilcock saw-mill cart.

Loading Hillaby's liquorice van on Back Street.

Emily Money's prize-winning fancy dress, *c.* 1935. The whole outfit was made of liquorice!

Mixing all-sorts. Each shape and colour of sweet was made separately and then mixed together with a shovel.

Pontefract Salvation Army band musicians, probably in Spring Gardens. The Jarrow Marchers were given food and were billeted here when they passed through Pontefract in October 1936 on their way to London.

Churches and Schools

Micklegate Wesleyan chapel, Horsefair, built in 1824. Note the gates mounted on wheels.

Hanging the new peal of bells at St Giles's church in June 1920, to commemorate peace at the end of the First World War. The ten bells were mainly made by melting down the previous eight that had been installed for Queen Victoria's Jubilee in 1887.

Christmas at St Giles's church. Note the box pews, balcony and plaster ceiling. The view dates to before 1868.

The organ at St Giles's church, also before 1868.

St Mary's Mission, Watergate, *c.* 1900.

Primitive Methodist Mission, Tanshelf, *c.* 1890.

Tom Haythorne and Charlie Fox restoring
the finials of All Saints' church, *c.* 1930.

Salvationist Joe Storey of the
Featherstone Corps.

The Friends meeting house and the Quaker burial ground on Harropwell Lane. The meeting house was built in 1697 and demolished in 1948.

A crocodile of children crossing Halfpenny Lane in around 1930, using a rope for safety. Note the future local historian, Harry Battye, holding a cane.

The King's School, which was housed in Pontefract's military depot on Back Northgate from 1890 to 1932.

Sports day at the King's School, c. 1930. All the school buildings except for the gatehouse were demolished in 1990 to make way for a supermarket.

The King's School football club in the 1911/12 season.

Mr J.G. Norton with the 1922/3 sixth form at the King's School. Note the ornate windows.

Laying the foundation stone of the Pontefract and District Girls' High School, 2 July 1910.

The hall and gymnasium of the Pontefract and District Girls' High School, c. 1930.

Pupils of Jefferson's School in the garden of Micklegate House where it was housed, *c*. 1870.

Miss Rennard's School, Tanshelf, *c*. 1886.

Mayor W. Barber opening the domestic science room at Willow Park School in 1945.

Jim Hepworth and his class at Northgate Boys' School, pre-1913.

Bert Forrest and his wife posing in front of the tobacconist's shop which they opened on Wakefield Road when he returned, maimed, from the First World War.

SECTION EIGHT
War and Peace

The Waterloo Monument was built of brick in 1818. Locally it was known as the Cranky Pin because of the curve it developed, and it had to be demolished in 1946. These fields are now Chequerfield Circle.

Butcher Clayton of Market Place in his Pontefract Volunteers uniform.

The warrant officers, staff sergeants and sergeants of 51st and 65th Regimental Districts at Pontefract Barracks, 26 April 1904.

Massive Crimean War guns at Pontefract Castle. The Castle ruins were turned into a park in the 1880s and also served as an open air museum for stonework, guns and even a tank.

Local volunteer soldiers photographed in front of a thatched shelter at Pontefract Castle before their posting to South Africa to serve in the second Boer War in 1899.

Tank No. 289 was awarded to Pontefract in 1919 in recognition of the money that was raised locally for the war effort. It was partly cut up for scrap in 1924 and is seen here in 1934 being removed to Nevison's Leap where it survived for some years.

The inauguration of the War Memorial by Mayor Richard Husband in 1923.

Crowds gather at Town End for the inauguration of the War Memorial in 1923.

Lighting bollards were placed around the War Memorial in response to the increase in traffic.

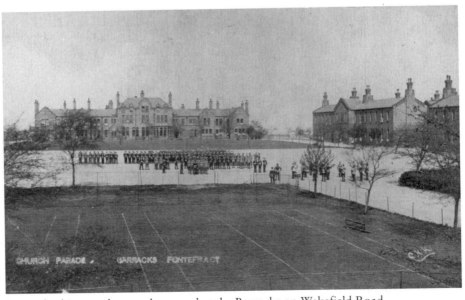

Square bashing on the parade ground at the Barracks on Wakefield Road.

Mayor T.J. Sides and Corporation staff at the peace celebrations on 19 July 1919.

The Barracks' gates, Wakefield Road.

Two sets of soldiers' kit ready for inspection.

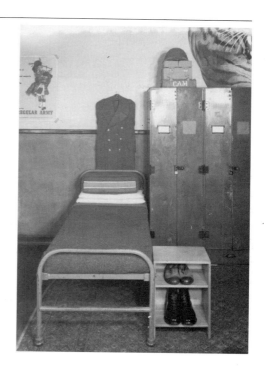

A soldier's place in Pontefract Barracks.

Land Army women 'ratting' in the Second World War to save crops from rodents.

THE CONTENTS OF THIS
UNEXPLODED BOMB
HAVE BEEN REMOVED
REFILL with CONTRIBUTIONS
LOCAL PRISONERS OF WAR COMFORTS FUND

The unexploded bomb which fell on Mayor's Walk, 8 August 1942.

Florence Desmond, 'star of stage and screen', helping to boost fund-raising for the war effort.

A military band drumming up financial support for the war effort, *c.* 1942.

Special constables simulating a road accident in a classroom before the eagle eye of an inspector with a clipboard. Note the staged argument in the background and the broken bottle.

Demolition of blast walls built to protect Pontefract General Infirmary, *c.* 1945.

A street party to celebrate VE Day in 1945.

Lance-Corporal and Mrs Eric Redsell, of Market Place. This newspaper photograph was entitled 'How to welcome a husband home after five years in enemy hands'.

Bullock's bus on the tilt test in the depot off Cornmarket.

SECTION NINE

Transport

After the service at St Giles's church on a Sunday morning in 1905. Soldiers from the Barracks marched to church led by the regimental band. One wealthy parishioner is being collected in an elegant early motor car.

Mr S. Hirst, liquorice manufacturer, with his tricycle, *c*. 1890.

Dr Blomfield (senior), *c*. 1905.

A hearse and taxis belonging to J.W. Marshall and Co. outside St Giles's church. The company advertised their 24-hour service with the motto 'We never sleep'.

A Ferrybridge Motor Co. van also photographed in front of St Giles's church.

Oswald Holmes and family posing on their bicycles in the snicket behind the printing works off Gillygate. Note the bricks used to prop up the bicycles to enable the photograph to be taken.

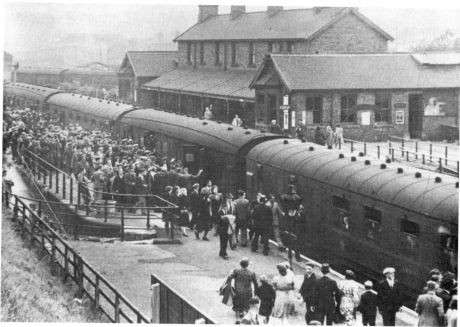

Race crowds at Baghill station, *c.* 1950.

The old Tanshelf station in the days of steam. This L&YR 0–6–0 No. 214 engine is conveying stone.

Baghill station with the LMS Patriot engine No. 45519, *Lady Godiva*, in the summer of 1960. Racing pigeons are about to be loaded into the guard's van and All Saints' church can be seen in the distance.

A studio portrait of an AA man who is standing on what looks like the sheepskin rug that would have been used for baby photography.

Mr Hemmingway, station master at Tanshelf station, c. 1920.

Mayor F.W. Lane and Corporation staff boarding a chartered double-decker bus for the customary church service at All Saints' on the last Sunday of the municipal year, November 1944.

A tram on Market Place. Pontefract's first tram ran on 29 October 1906 and the last on 1 November 1925. Note the dome on the New Elephant Hotel on the right.

A new ambulance, probably standing in front of the infirmary wing of the workhouse.

A bus standing in front of Bullock & Sons Ltd, Cornmarket, *c.* 1920.

Fleet of buses belonging to South Yorkshire Motors. Note the War Memorial has not yet moved from Town End.

Principal boy at the Assembly Rooms.

Leisure

The gates and gatehouses at the entrance to Pontefract Park and the racecourse. The gatehouses were later rebuilt.

The brick pond inside the Park gates, *c.* 1920.

A distant view of the Park lake and boathouse.

A charabanc at the Park gates.

Pontefract Borough Band, Pontefract Castle, *c.* 1895.

Tennis at the Barracks on Wakefield Road.

Bowling at Pontefract Park, *c.* 1910.

Serious cricket enthusiasts at the club on Beechnut Lane, off Colonel's Walk, *c.* 1910.
Note the trophies on the bench.

The son of the publican, Mr Wilson, at the New Inn, *c*. 1920.

The old Windmill Inn on Wool Market, *c*. 1910. It was later rebuilt using attractive terracotta.

An interior view of the lounge at the Queen's Hotel, *c*. 1930. Note the Lloyd loom chairs and the landscapes painted on the walls.

Pontefract water polo team at the Headlands baths in 1936.

Pontefract Swimming Club with the baths' manager, Mr Colley, *c*. 1930.

A tug of war team, probably at the Prince of Wales Colliery, *c.* 1910. Note the very short haircuts with the longer forelock to make keeping clean easier after working at the pit.

Pontefract Rugby Club, winners of the Yorkshire Challenge Cup 1890–1.

Pontefract Victoria Northern Union Football Club in the 1909/10 season.

The Pontefract 'Rocks' in the 1908/9 season.

The cast of *Dick Whittington* posing in a charabanc in front of the Assembly Rooms, *c.* 1920.

The Da Capo Melody Makers at the Assembly Rooms, *c.* 1930.

The Assembly Rooms soon after the opening by Lord Fitzwilliam in January 1883. Note the ornate decoration round the stage.

'Harnie's Variety of Thrills – a new ride for 1937.' This photograph was taken at the Statutes Fair.

'Hal Denver – Ladies can see this performance without being offended or insulted.' This photograph was taken at the Statutes Fair, *c.* 1930.

A showman's trailer in front of the built-up Midland Road leading to Baghill station, *c.* 1920.

Children blowing bubbles in Love Lane, *c.* 1950.

The artist Percy Rhodes and his two brothers. Despite the loss of two fingers in a shooting accident, he was a prolific illustrator for local author J.S. Fletcher.

Richard Holmes (seated), historian and printer, having tea with his family and pets, *c*. 1910.

George Pennington, architect, enjoying the garden with his family, *c*. 1910. Note the bear on wheels.

The Castle, *c.* 1890, before the sloping road to the central lawn was built and trees were planted. Note the cannon and the flagpole. The custodian is seated in the foreground.

Looking down from the Castle keep towards the Booths and All Saints' church, *c.* 1890.

The keep from the sallyport, *c.* 1890.

Planting trees outside the Castle walls, *c.* 1890.

The bandstand at the Castle in 1932.

The Castle terrace with trees and shrubs, *c*. 1930.

The ornamental bridge across the Castle kitchens, *c.* 1890.

Mr Firth, 'curator' of the Castle, photographed in the centre of a group of friends, *c.* 1910.

The Castle kitchens planted up as a rose garden, 1936.

The royal apartments at the Castle were romantically overgrown by 1942.

St Clement's chapel laid out with flowerbeds and circled with trees in 1923.

The Castle entrance and the bar leading down Castle Garth in 1930.

The Castle Museum, *c.* 1920. Note the man-trap under the table.

The Castle Museum, *c.* 1920.

Frank Holmes holding human bones from St Richard's friary, found during the construction of the Edward VII extension at Pontefract General Infirmary in 1924.

Alf Ward and his young helpers excavating the tomb recess in the Lady Chapel of All Saints' church, c. 1950.

Archaeology before it was professionalized: a stone coffin being excavated at St John's priory, *c.* 1957.

Dr Blomfield's garden arch was constructed out of fragments of stone from St John's.

Perilous attempts at aerial photography were made during excavations at St John's, *c.* 1957.

Hanging coronation decorations on the Market Hall in 1936. Note the remodelled plain pediment.

SECTION ELEVEN

People and Events

The huge bonfire on Park Hill was part of the peace celebrations in 1919.

This coronation bonfire, built by Mr J. Hanson in 1911, rose 36 ft high and was 11 ft across.

The funeral procession of Mayor Richard Husband, who died in office in 1923. The cortège is coming down Mill Hill.

Lord Baden-Powell at Pontefract Castle in 1930. He returned to the racecourse in 1933 for an all-Yorkshire Scout rally and was made a Freeman of the Borough.

The Princess Royal inspecting Girl Guides in front of the Town Hall in 1925.

A horse pulling a lifeboat up Horsefair, presumably to raise money. Pontefract had already financed a lifeboat, the *Pomfret and Goole*, which was launched at Ferrybridge on 2 December 1865.

Celebrations marking the coronation of George V in 1910. Note the arch leading into Ropergate and the fact that Valley Road had not yet been cut.

'Support the Pageant and help Pontefract Infirmary', *c.* 1920. Note the barefooted child on the right hand edge.

'Hip Hip, Hoorah!' The proclamation of Edward VIII read by Mayor T.J. Sides in January 1936. Note the black armbands of mourning for George V.

'To feed 1,800 of Pomfret's Distress Children.' Gathering food during the General Strike of 1926. The Town Hall can be seen to the right and the door to the prison cells is behind the lorry driver.

Over 1,500 St John Ambulancemen from the Yorkshire region parading up Horsefair in 1924.

Local St John Ambulancemen, with Mr Amery in charge, in front of Headlands Road baths in 1924.

Ewbank's car and cycle showroom at the junction of Wakefield Road and Mill Hill. Note the circular water trough around the lamp post.

Ewbank's was gutted by fire on 26 September 1923.

The ceremony held in 1933 when Great Northern House on Salter Row was handed over to Pontefract General Infirmary to become an extension for convalescents. The matron, Miss Fanny Thompson, known as Aunty Fanny Thompson, is on the left.

The crowds in Market Place mourning the death of Edward VII in 1910.

The cake made at Johnson's bakery in 1937 to celebrate the first anniversary of the Alexandra Theatre as a cinema.

Geoffrey Marr of Pontefract, Captain of the *Queen Mary*, who later became Commodore of the Cunard fleet.

The collapse of Holmes' printers on 17 July 1906 as a result of explosives used to make cellars next door.

The Duchess of York welcomed by the matron of Pontefract General Infirmary, 1928.

The cake made to celebrate Geoffrey Marr's captaincy of the *Queen Mary*.

A cake made in Pontefract to celebrate the ascent of Everest in 1953.

A steam traction engine was used to bring Darrington residents into Pontefract to celebrate the coronation of Edward VII in 1901. Note the construction of Blackburn's, later Burton's.

The Prince of Wales and Mayor J.J. Frain visiting a recreational centre for the unemployed at Baghill House in 1933.

Farm horse crossing the floods on Knottingley Road in 1933.

Flooding on Knottingley Road in 1933.

Acknowledgements

Wakefield Metropolitan District Council Leisure Services: Museums, Galleries and Castles are grateful for the generous gifts, loans and documentation provided by:

Mr S. Appleyard • Mr E. Archer • Geo. Bassett & Co. (Wilkinson's)
Mr H. Battye • Mr J. Booth • Mrs E. Brooks • Dr H. Burnett
Mrs K. Canning • Mr S. Clark • Mr P. Cookson • Mr C.P. Dearden
Mrs W. Eaton • Mr H. Gelder • Mrs M. Glasby • G. & J. Hall Ltd
Mr Hanson • Mr T. Hawley • Mr and Mrs D. Hewes • Mrs M. Hill
Mr F. Holmes • Mr J. Holmes • Mrs M. Horner • Mr E. Houlder
Mr G. Jackson • Mr J. Johnson • Mr Kitson • Mrs R. Leadbeater
Mrs A. Lightowler • Mr H. Limbert • Mr D. Lodge • Mrs J.B. Loftus
Mr Lovett • Mr J. Marshall • Mr M. Martin • Mr J. Maud
Mr Parker • *Pontefract Advertiser* • Pontefract and District Archaeological
Society Pontefract Library • Mr Reid • Royal Commission on the Historical
Monuments of England • Mrs Savage • Miss C. Somerville • Mr B. Tyson
Wakefield Metropolitan District Council Social Services Department
Miss B. Webster • Mrs M. Waiter • Mrs Whincup • Mr J. Whitehead
Mr E. Whitlock • Mr D. Wilcox • Miss A. Williams
Yorkshire Weekly Newspaper Group Ltd • *Yorkshire Post* and many others.